INDIAN TALES

OF THE GREAT ONES

INDIAN TALES OF THE GREAT ONES

Among Men, Women, and Bird-people

Cornelia Sorabji

With Illustrations by Warwick Goble

GYAN

Published by

GYAN

Gyan Publishing House
5, Ansari Road
Daryaganj, New Delhi-110002
Phone: 011-47034999, 9811692060
E-mail: books@gyanbooks.com

Distribution Network
gyanbooks.com
India, USA, Canada, UK, Australia, France

ISBN : 978-81-212-9757-8 (PB)
First Published, 1916

2nd Impression 2023

Printed at: Gyan Press, Delhi.

INDIAN TALES OF THE GREAT ONES
Author: CORNELIA SORABJI

C 797

NAILA

(See page 64)

INDIAN TALES OF THE GREAT ONES

Among Men, Women, and Bird-people

By Cornelia Sorabji

With Illustrations by Warwick Goble

To

my Baby-Friends

in

all Worlds

CONTENTS

INDIAN TALES OF THE GREAT ONES

The Eagle Brothers

There were once two great brother-eagles—Jattayu and Sanpati. And Jattayu was King of all the Eagle Tribes; and among the birds of the air there was none more powerful than Jattayu.

The brothers lived together on a crag of the mountains called the Home of Snow, which stretch across the north-east boundary of India.

They lived there because there was no higher spot in all the world that could be found for their home. And day after day Jattayu ranged the air, marshalling his bird-armies, or settling disputes, or swooping down on the things which he sought for food—for all the bird-people belonged to Jattayu, and owed him allegiance even with their lives, if so he should desire.

And Jattayu was strong and took what he willed, without making excuse.

And Jattayu was feared, even though there were those among the bird-people who could tell how Jattayu could be gentle to the weak.

And of these was his brother Sanpati.

When Jattayu ranged the air, he was a king; but when he flew back on strong outspread wing to his home in the snow mountains, he was only the big brother of Little-Eagle Sanpati.

And together as children they shared the day's meal, and together

The Eagle Brothers

as children they talked of the wonders of the heavens. And always and always in their talk Little-Eagle Sanpati noticed one yearning in the big brother whom he loved and admired.

"I want to get to the sun. Oh, as near as I can!" said Big-Brother Jattayu.

And day after day Little-Eagle Sanpati kept wondering how this could be managed.

And his love for Jattayu was so great that it found a way.

"If one should fly between him and the sun to protect him," he said, "it could be done."

So, one day he made the little-eagle heart of him very brave, and made Jattayu believe that he too was wanting to see the sun; but that he was afraid of falling back upon the earth in terror, when he got near the sun's brilliance. So he begged Jattayu to fly just under him to protect him.

And Jattayu consented; and they circled, Little-Eagle Sanpati and Big-Brother Jattayu, higher and higher, till they got so near to the sun that even Jattayu had had enough, and turned to fly back to the safe quiet nest in the white earth mountains, taking Little-Eagle Sanpati with him.

"It is wonderful," he kept saying, "that I got so near, and yet was not struck or burnt by the Sun-God and the fierceness of his rays. It is a tale of wonder for all the bird-people to hear. Well was it, Little-Eagle Sanpati, that I was there when you fell on my back in terror."

And in Little-Eagle Sanpati's heart was a great gladness that Jattayu had had his desire. Nor did Jattayu, nor anyone in all the bird-world, know the reason why Little-Eagle Sanpati from that day forward remained the home-stay eagle who could not fly.

It was because in protecting Big-Brother Jattayu whom he loved, from the rays of the sun, poor Little-Eagle Sanpati's wings had all been scorched away.

The Throne of Justice

Long before time as we count it, there lived in India a great and just King whose name was Vikramaditya. When he died, his beautiful palace and city of marble fell into ruins: and people remembered nothing but his name, and that he was great and good, and wise and gentle.

One day, some boys who were minding cows led them near a green mound among the ruins: and while the cows cropped the grass, the boys played.

And one of them invented this game.

"I shall be the Judge," he said, "and you shall bring your quarrels to me. I will do justice."

So he sat on the mound; and the boys ran away and whispered, and made a tale of wrong, and brought it to the boy on the mound, who did justice.

But the odd thing was, that the "justice" was such wisdom, that even through their play, the boys felt that something wonderful had happened to their playfellow.

"He is a real Judge, not a play Judge," was what they said.

And they told their parents; and soon all the village got into the habit of coming to the boy on the mound to settle disputes. And everyone was always sure that his judgment was right.

Now there lived close to the ruined city, a King great and powerful: and to his ears also came the story of the boy doing justice on the green mound. And the King laughed and said, "Why, he is sitting on the seat of Vikramaditya; that is why he is wise."

Then the King began to wish the throne for himself. And he sent men with pickaxes and shovels, who dug away the boy's green mound. Deeper and deeper they went, till they came to a throne of black marble, resting on the backs of twenty-four beautiful carved eagles of marble. And the throne was taken to the palace of the King, and a great day of rejoicing was proclaimed, when the King would mount the throne.

On the great day the King came in state, with his mace bearers, and the men who called his titles, and the men who carried the State jewels, and the men who fanned him with great fans made of the green-blue eyes of a peacock's tail.

But when the King would have mounted the throne, one of the carven eagles which bore the throne on its

One of the carven eagles came alive

back, came alive and spoke to the King.

"Stop!" he said. "Have you never wanted for yourself the kingdom of another?"

And the King had to own that he had.

"Then fast and pray for three days," said the eagle, "and come back again."

And the eagle flew away.

And after three days the King returned; but the second eagle stopped him.

"Have you never", he said, "done harm to another, to rob him of his riches?"

And the King said, "Yes—often."

"Then fast and pray for three days," said the eagle, "and come again."

And so each time that the King returned to mount the throne, an eagle spoke and showed some evil of his life, and the King went away sorrowful to his three days' fasting.

And last of all there was only one eagle left; and the King came walking slowly: "This time I must sit on the throne," was his thought.

But "Stop!" said likewise this eagle also, "unless you can tell me that your heart is as pure as the heart of a child."

And the King looked within, and found his heart not as the heart of a child.

"I am not worthy," said the King.

But he knew that the last eagle had solved the mystery of the green mound of grass. The throne of Vikramaditya, where the shepherd boy did justice, was denied to him, the great and mighty King.

For he who would be perfectly just, must have the heart of a little child.

Samyukta, or
The Story of the Own-choosing.

Samyukta, daughter of the King of Kanauj, was the most beautiful Princess in all India. And Prithi Raja, the King of Delhi, wanted to marry her.

He knew that it would not be easy, because her father was his enemy. However, always and always he liked best to do what was not easy to do. So he meant to try.

First he sought out her old nurse, who lived not far from the palace. Touching her feet with his forehead, as is the way of saluting mother-people, he asked her advice. The old woman loved Prithi Raja very dearly, and found a way of helping him.

"Give me", she said, "that picture

which the great painter at Delhi has made of you, on ivory, in green and gold: and the rest I will tell you when I come again from my journey."

And the nurse who loved Prithi Raja, went a long way till she came to the gates of the palace of Kanauj. She asked to see the Queen. Now it happened that at that moment, the Queen wanted a new waiting-woman for the Princess. So she took the nurse, and gave her to the household of the Princess.

Samyukta, the Princess, was indeed beautiful. Good was she also, and of a true heart. And as the old woman brushed her hair, or sat out with her on the roof-balcony on the still, hot nights when the Princess was sleepless, she told her tales of Prithi Raja, King of Delhi, and of his great love for Samyukta.

And she showed Samyukta his picture painted on ivory in green and gold. And as the Princess looked on his face, her heart went out to meet the heart of the King who loved her.

And presently the King of Kanauj said: "It is time for the Swayamvara" —that is the choosing of her husband by a Princess-Lady. And he sent his heralds to all parts of India, to call the princes of India to the great choosing.

But to his enemy, Prithi Raja, the King of Delhi, he sent no message. Nevertheless the King of Delhi came to the choosing, he and his friend, disguised as minstrels.

And the palace courtyard was gay and ready for the choosing. Garlands of roses and jasmine hung from the pillars, and garlands of yellow mari-

Lightly she held the garland

golds. The King and Queen sat on golden thrones on a marble balcony: and down below were the thrones of the princes who sought the hand of Samyukta.

Each prince had his men-at-arms and his heralds; and all were dressed in jewels and cloth of gold. And the musicians sat in a watch-tower at the gate: and all who came and went, and all that happened, they saw best of all. And with the musicians sat Prithi Raja, the great prince.

And now the bugles sounded: and Samyukta came from the inner courtyard. She wore a sari that flowed about her like golden water, and the golden anklets on her feet and the golden bracelets on her arms tinkled music. Her eyes were on the ground as she walked, and lightly she held the garland of fresh jasmine flowers, which she would place on the neck of him whom she chose to be her husband.

As she reached the outer courtyard, she raised her eyes, and then she saw a wooden figure of Prithi Raja standing in the place of the King's door-keeper. And she knew that her father had done this thing to hurt Prithi Raja, the true knight of her heart.

From that moment her choice was made. Proudly she walked past one prince after another. Proudly and patiently she heard the long tale of his greatness sounded by the heralds: and silently and proudly she passed on.

There was but one prince left, he who sat near the door-keeper. What would she do? The King and Queen leaned out of their marble balcony, and all the great crowd watched breathless.

But the last prince also did Samyukta reject, and turning to the wooden image of Prithi Raja, who had had no invitation to the Great-Choosing, she placed on its neck the garland, kept for her true knight alone.

Then was there a clash of steel, as the King and all the princes rose in wrath. Surely for this insult Samyukta would now be bound in chains and sent to the deepest dungeon of the palace.

But quicker than wrath was love. Prithi Raja the Minstrel, mounted on Prithi Raja the King's swiftest charger, was at her side, and stooping lifted her to his saddle, and rode away swiftly to the gates of Delhi.

And this was in the days long ago, when men were knights and fought for their ladies, and did with their own hand the thing which was not easy to do.

The Man who made himself an Archer

There was a Master-Archer whose name was Drona: and it was he who taught all the princes of India to shoot, so that none could conquer them.

Now he was jealous for the honour of the princes. And there came to him one named Ekalavya, the king of a caste that was not the soldier-caste, who said: "Teach me to shoot."

But Drona made answer: "You are not of the knightly caste. I cannot teach you." For he was afraid that the low-caste man might become the equal of the high-born princes.

Then Ekalavya went away very sadly to the forest, and built a shrine to Drona, the Master-Archer. And he thought about him, and fasted and prayed night and day for skill in shooting: and night and day he practised ceaselessly, shooting arrows into the distance—shooting and shooting. And he forgot the riches of his palace and all the pleasures of the world, in reaching out to his great desire.

One day Drona and the high-born princes were out shooting in the forest, and they had with them a dog. And the dog strayed from the princes and lost his way, barking in the darkness for his masters, not far from the shrine of Ekalavya.

And Ekalavya heard, and shot an arrow in the direction of the sound; and the arrow went straight into the dog's mouth.

And the dog ran howling to his masters. And they were very angry; for said they, "Someone who can shoot has sent this arrow into the dog's

Ekalavya at the shrine

mouth." And they made the dog show them the way to the shrine, and there was Ekalavya shooting ceaselessly.

"Who are you," said the princes, "who have skill in shooting even as ourselves?"

"I am Ekalavya," said he, "a pupil of the great Master-Archer Drona."

So the princes went and told Drona, and he came back with them to the shrine in the forest.

"How say you," said Drona, "that you are my pupil?"

"Because I have taught myself to shoot, thinking only of you and your great skill in shooting."

Then said Drona, "If you are my pupil, give me the fee due to a Master."

"Most gladly," said Ekalavya, a great joy in his face. "Ask what you will. I have nothing I would not give with all my heart."

"Is that true?" said Drona. "Well then, I ask the thumb of your right hand."

And Ekalavya, allowing no look of sadness to spoil his gift, cut off his thumb, without a word, and laid it at the feet of the Master-Archer. But

Drona spurned it, and walked away.

Then Ekalavya turned again to his shooting. But he found that, with the loss of his thumb, his skill had gone for ever.

So were the great ones left without a rival.

But in Heaven the Gods said, "Ekalavya is truly of the knightly caste: and men knew it not."

The Blue Bird and the Archer

One day Drona, the Master-Archer, made trial of the skill of the princes his pupils. He had them all out before him together.

"Take your bows and arrows," said he, "and be ready to shoot, when I tell you, at the blue bird in yonder tree."

Prince Yudhisthira, being the eldest, was called first.

"Be ready to shoot," said Drona. "But tell me first what you see. Do you see the bird?"

"Yes," said Yudhisthira.

"What else do you see? Myself, your brothers, or the tree?"

"I see yourself, my brothers, the tree, and the bird."

Three times Drona asked this question, and three times was he thus answered. Then very sorrowfully he turned from Yudhisthira. Not by him was the bird to be shot.

Prince after prince, he questioned on this wise; and all alike made answer: "I see you, my brothers, the tree, and the bird."

And now there was but one prince left, Arjun, the master's favourite pupil.

"Tell me, Arjun, with bow bent, what do you see?"

"I see a bird."

"Do you not see myself, your brothers, the tree?"

"I see the bird alone," said Arjun, "not you, nor the tree, nor my brothers."

"Of what colour is the bird?"

"I see only a bird's head."

"Then shoot," said Drona joyfully; and even as he expected, as soon as the arrow sped from the bow, the bird was headless.

Draupadi and the Great Game

When Arjun grew to be a man, one of his first battles was against a King called Drupada. He and his four brothers, the Pandavas as they were called, put their soldiers in a ring round King Drupada's fortress, and let no one pass out or go in.

In a week all the King's servants were dead: and the brothers marched into the palace and took all that they wanted of gold and emeralds, of horses and chariots. The lady Draupadi also, the King's daughter, became theirs by the rules of war.

And Draupadi lived happily with her mother-in-law and the princes.

And all went well, till an enemy of the brothers, jealous of their happiness and their power, tempted Yudhisthira, the eldest of the five. He challenged him to a game of chance in which he put down all he possessed, to lose or win. And Yudhisthira lost. He lost his palace, his chariots and horses, and his whole kingdom. He lost his brothers and himself, and last of all he lost Draupadi also.

Draupadi was the most beautiful of women, and Yudhisthira's enemy was glad indeed when she was brought captive before him. But he was also afraid; for there was something so free in the spirit of Draupadi, that he knew it would not be well with the man who made her a slave.

So, thinking it were wiser to be content with the kingdom and let Draupadi go—

"Ask," he said, "a boon, and it shall be granted."

"I ask then," said Draupadi, "for the freedom of Yudhisthira."

"Granted," said the enemy, for he did not dare break his word. But he marvelled that she did not ask for herself; so, "Ask again" he said.

"Ask", he said, "a boon, and it shall be granted"

"And for the freedom of his brothers with their weapons and chariots of war."

"It is granted: but I give you a third boon. Will you not ask for your own freedom?"

"By no means," said Draupadi. "The Pandavas, armed and free, can conquer the world. It is they who will rescue me. They need owe nothing to a boon; nor, with the Pandavas free, need I either, any longer."

The Self-Blinding

Everyone knows the name of Dhritarashtra, the uncle of the five great soldier-men, the Pandavas.

Dhritarashtra was blind; and Dhritarashtra was alone in his blindness.

And when Gandhari, his bride, saw the hurt of his loneliness—"Let me in to him behind his bars of darkness," she said to the gods.

And she bound her eyes tightly; and day and night were alike to her for ever. But Dhritarashtra was no more lonely in his night of sightlessness.

The Story of the Maiden-Knight

Drupada, the King of the Panchalas, had prayed for a son, that he might destroy his enemy the Master-Archer.

But his wife was childless. Then as he still prayed and prayed, Shiva appeared to him and told him that he should have a son who should first be a daughter.

And in due time a daughter was born to him. But the Queen said, "She is a son;" and so great was her faith that she prevailed on the King to proclaim the child a son, and to perform the son-ceremonies.

And the child was called Shikhandi. And she grew strong and beautiful: but was seen of none save her parents and her faithful nurse.

All too soon it was time for her to be married. And again by the advice of the Queen, they sought for her the most beautiful princess in all India. "We must believe the word of the gods," said the Queen.

But at last the secret was known, and the King whose daughter was sought in marriage was very angry. "I have", he said, "been insulted;" and he prepared to make war on the Panchalas.

And Shikhandi's father felt that he had done wrong, and had been deceitful: and he was afraid.

But Shikhandi's mother said, "We only relied on the word of the gods. Be unafraid as I am unafraid: and prepare to defend the kingdom. She shall be a son."

And Shikhandi, sad at heart that she was the cause of all this trouble, wandered forth to lose herself. "If I am not here any longer, the King and my father will make peace," was what she said in her heart.

And, wandering, she came to a great forest, and to a great house the doors of which were open. And the house smelt of smoke and incense, and yet no one was there: and it seemed to have a host, and yet was hostless.

And Shikhandi sat down in the house, and brooded, heeding not time nor self, in her great desire to save her people.

And to her presently came the kind Yakshas, whose the palace was, and he asked her what she wished.

"Make me a man," said she, "a perfect man. My father is about to be destroyed: and if I were a man this would not happen. Make me, oh, Yakshas! a man: and let me keep

She came to a great house

that manhood till my father is saved."

And the Yakshas was moved with pity: and gave her his manhood and his mighty form, till she should fulfil her object. So she went forth a warrior, in the form of Sthuna, the Yakshas.

And the King of Wealth, coming that way, found Sthuna the woman sitting alone in the palace: and between laughter and disgust—"You shall remain a woman," he said. But later he was sorry, and he added—"Till Shikhandi's death."

So was fulfilled the promise of Shiva—"She shall be first a daughter: and then a son, Shikhandi, Maiden-Knight."

And the mother of Shikhandi was full of a great gladness, that she had believed the word of the gods.

The Way of Friendship

Simple is the way of friendship.

Make a fire of two sticks, or twenty, or two hundred—any number will do: and if you walk round the fire sunwise, with that one whom you would have for a friend, the gods themselves will not take back the gift.

And this was the lesson which Drona tried to teach King Drupada. Drona was the Master-Archer as we know, and Drupada was King of the Panchalas. Now Drupada was not worthy of friendship, for he did not believe that two sticks would do for the lighting of the Fire of Friendship.

"They must be two hundred," said Drupada, "and of the most costly wood."

And Drona was sad: for he was a

poor man, and two sticks gathered in a wood were all that he could bring to the lighting.

"And you will bring one of the two," he had said to Drupada; "for all that matters is that we should bring the same."

But Drupada shook his head.

And Drona journeyed to a far country, and for many years the River of Time flowed between him and the man whom he wanted for friend.

And at last they were once again on the same bank of the river. And Drona's pupils, Arjun and his brother princes, took Drupada captive and brought him to Drona.

And Drona said: "I will teach Drupada the way of friendship. Since my two sticks, to one of which he is welcome, will not do for the lighting of the fire, he shall give me half his two hundred sticks of the costliest wood."

And of all Drupada's riches—treasure of gold and emeralds and diamonds and pearls, strings of camels and horses

Drona and the Fire of Friendship

and elephants, chariots of war and houses and slaves—he made two equal parts; and one part he gave to Drupada and one part he kept for himself, that he might begin the teaching of the way of friendship to the man who was not worthy to learn the way.

Sibi Rana and the Grey Dove

Long and long ago there lived a King called Sibi Rana. He was known to all the world as a man who protected the weak, but who yet did not withhold that which might belong to the strong.

So nearly perfect was he that the gods asked the greatest God to test his goodness.

And this was the way of the testing.

One day as the King sat in his great Hall of Justice, there came in at the window a poor frightened grey dove, nearly spent with flight, and flew straight against the heart of the King. Looking up, the King saw an eagle in pursuit, and without a moment's hesitation he opened his white robes to shelter the dove.

The eagle turned its piercing eye

Sibi Rana and the Dove

upon the King. "So this, then, is your justice," he said. "You rob me of my food."

"Nay," said the King, "on the contrary, food equal in weight to the bird shall be given to you."

"Whatever food I desire?"

"Yes, whatever you desire."

"But if I desire your own flesh?"

"My flesh shall be given," said the King.

"Then I wish the weight of the bird to be taken from your right side, and in the presence of the Queen and your small son," demanded the eagle.

"Beseech the Queen to come hither," said the King, "with my son."

And to the horror of all the Court, the scales were brought; and in the presence of the Queen they prepared to slice off the weight of the bird from the King's right side.

The King sat steadfast: but alas! the bird seemed to grow heavier, with each fresh gift of the King's flesh.

And the eagle watched from the foot of the throne: and the eagle laughed aloud.

Then from the left eye of the King fell a single tear.

"Stay," said the eagle, "I want no unwilling sacrifice."

"Nay, but," said the King, "willing enough is this. My left eye but weeps because to the right side of the King alone is it given to protect the weak and defenceless."

Upon which, says the old story, the miracle happened. For even the eagle saw the beauty of giving: and he flew away hungry to his mountains, and neither was the King really hurt, nor the dove without a home.

The Crow and the Bell of Justice

This story is told of one Anangapal, who ruled in Delhi, and who loved justice.

He caused two great lions of stone to be placed near his palace gates, where all could see them. A bell hung from the bar between the lions. Whoever struck that bell claimed justice, and got justice of Anangapal the King.

One day a crow swung in the breeze on the tongue of the bell, and the cry for justice clanged forth, reaching the ear of the King.

"Who strikes the bell?" he asked.

"My lord, it is a crow."

"Let justice be done," said Anangapal.

"What asks the crow?"

But no one could tell. So the King himself read the message.

"The crow strikes my bell, between the mouths of my stone lions. See you not? The crow came as is its habit, to pick morsels of food out of the mouth of the lion. And the lions were not lions. I deceived the crow. Let a sheep be killed: and place some meat in the lions' mouths, that the crow may find its meal."

So did even the least of his subjects get justice and bounty at the hands of Anangapal the Just.

Raziya, Queen of Delhi

Raziya was the daughter of Altamish, one of the Moghul slave-kings of Delhi who lived in the thirteenth century. She is the only woman besides our own Queen Victoria who has ruled Delhi.

Altamish had sons also; but when he was dying he said: "You will find no one better fitted to rule the kingdom than my daughter Raziya."

And after his nobles had suffered for some time the cruelty and injustice of Raziya's half-brother, they began to see that the King was right.

And Raziya herself helped them.

The King had given order that anyone who had a petition to make should appear at the great Mosque in Delhi, on a Friday morning, wearing a coloured garment, and his petition would be heard forthwith.

Now, on a Friday morning when all the men worshippers, in their beautiful white garments, had assembled at the Mosque for the weekly prayer, Raziya made herself brave to go among them dressed in a veil of the Prophet's green—a figure whom none could miss.

And the people remembered the custom of the good King who had denied a hearing to no one; and they said: "The King's daughter is herself to-day a beggar." So they listened, making it easy for Raziya to speak.

And Raziya said: "My brother has killed his brother, and now he would slay me."

And all the people, as one man, vowed to help her. And Raziya was put upon the throne of Delhi.

Raziya and the Peasant

And Raziya ruled as few men have ruled in Delhi. She loved justice and mercy, and she gave both to her people. She led them to battle, pitching her own tent in the place of greatest danger: she was generous and wise, and entirely forgetful of her woman's self. All this her people knew of her; and all this historians have said of her.

But one old man, who wrote the longest tale of her gifts and virtues, tells us the reason of her failure to rule India: "She was a great monarch; but she was a woman, and she ruled as a man."

The Moslem people of those days could not forgive her that. They could not forgive her that, being a woman, she came before them with face unveiled; that, being a woman, she did successfully the work of a man, and asked no woman's reward. And so, though they took her love and protection for so long that they forgot the cruelty of her brother who had reigned before, they turned against her in the end and dethroned her, and put her in prison.

From prison later, she escaped, and led an army to regain her kingdom. And perhaps she might some day have won it back, but for a sad thing that befell her.

In the battle which she waged she was defeated, and fled alone to the jungles.

Passing through a field, she saw an old peasant at work, and begged for some food, for she was starving.

The man gave her a piece of bread, which she ate gladly; and then being worn out, she tied her horse to a tree and lay down in the field to take a short rest. She wore the dress of a man; but the peasant saw her jewels gleaming, as she slept unprotected in that lonely spot. He knew that she was a woman; and no more afraid of her, he killed her and buried her there, in a corner of a field outside the walls of that Delhi which she had ruled.

So Raziya lost her kingdom because she was not enough of a woman to make her people love a woman ruler; and she died, because she was a woman, and without protection.

And her story is told here, for the reason that we know now that the old historian was wrong; and that a woman need not fail even in the great work of a sovereign, only because she is a woman. Raziya failed because she thought that for success she must put aside her womanhood. Our Queen Victoria succeeded. And one of the things which we know that she gave to her people was that same great heart of a woman and a mother, which poor Raziya believed that she must slay.

Baber the Tiger

There was a Moghul boy-king, who fought his first battle when he was twelve years of age, and he won it, as he says himself, "thanks to the distinguished valour of my young soldiers".

But like the boys in fairy tales, he had wicked uncles, who made trouble for him; and before he was seventeen years old, he had won and lost two of his kingdoms.

This is the boy whom all the world knows by his nickname of "Baber the Tiger". And the most wonderful thing we know about him is his great spirit, which nothing could subdue. Success could not spoil him, and defeat could not make him hang his head.

Always did he find something in which to take pleasure.

Driven away from one of his early attempts to take Delhi, he has a race with two of his officers; and he writes of the first meal which he ate in hiding as of a royal banquet—"such peace and plenty, nice fat meat, bread of fine flour well baked, sweet melons, excellent grapes".

Again: "I could not, on account of one or two defeats, sit down and look idly around me", he tells us; and we find him getting to work again immediately.

Many years of wandering were before him. He had only two tents and less than three hundred followers. They had to bear thirst and hunger, pain and poverty; but the joyous spirit of the Tiger-boy carried them through all. And his tenderness and love and thoughtfulness were as his courage and good cheer.

He gave his own tent to his mother, who shared his wanderings; and for her, as for his followers, he gathered brightness from every smallest thing—from tulips and grasses, from animals and birds and insects.

Kabul fell to him when he was eighteen; and here for ten years he lived peacefully, caring for his mother and grandmother, his aunts and sisters, and all his people who had been faithful to him. Here also he married the lady whom he called "Maham"—"my Moon"—of whom we know only because of Baber's great love for her. It was the "Moon-Lady" who was the mother of Humayun.

But the land beyond the hills was calling Baber; and soon there came a chance to try once more for the throne of Delhi.

The people of Hindustan were fight-

Baber's Vow

ing among themselves, and asked Baber's help. Of the great battle that Baber won on the field of Paniput near Delhi, there are many stories.

"Battle was joined at the time of early morning prayers"; and by mid-day Baber the Tiger was lord of Delhi and Agra. There are wonderful tales of the presents which he sent after this victory, to his family and people in Kabul—forgetting no one. Ladies and nurses of the zenana, officers, clerks, traders, even "all who pray for me", were remembered; and so great was the list, that it was three days before the presents were divided. To his daughters and aunts and the princesses of the zenana were given gold plates full of gems, trays of coins, and nine different kinds of stuff chosen for each lady by Baber himself—"uplifting us with pride", says his daughter.

His last great campaign was against the Rajputs; and that was a fight worthy of the warrior who was now about forty-four years of age, and who had begun fighting when he was twelve. It was before this fight that he made "the Great Repentance".

When Baber was in Kabul he had learnt to drink wine, and had grown to be fond of this indulgence. Walking round his outposts, however, before the Rajput battle, the thought came to Baber that it would be good to mend his life now in this matter, so that he might have something to give in penitence to God.

And he sent immediately for his great goblets of gold and silver studded with precious stones; and there on the battle-field he had them broken to pieces and given to the poor, vowing that he would never drink wine again.

That night and the next, three hundred of his nobles did likewise, pouring upon the ground the wine which they had brought with them. So, "having knocked on the door of Penitence", did they join battle. And once more victory was theirs.

The last tale which the books tell of Baber is beautiful.

He loved Humayun, the son of his Moon-Lady, as we know, with all his heart. And Humayun was ill.

Everything that the doctors could do, was done; but Humayun was sick unto death. Then a holy man said to Baber: "If some precious thing were given to God in exchange for Humayun, God might let him live."

And the holy man talked of the Kohinor, which Baber had got from Gwalior, and which is now in the crown of our King-Emperor of Britain.

But Baber, who more than anyone we know had loved being alive, said: "No, that is not the most precious thing I have to give. There is my life."

And he walked three times round Humayun's bed, saying: "Oh, God! if a life may be given for a life, I, who am Baber, I give my life and my being for Humayun." And he went away and prayed and fasted, saying many times: "I have borne it away. I have prevailed."

That night Baber fell ill, and Humayun began to get better. Then Baber called his nobles together, and charged them to serve Humayun faithfully, for he himself would rule no more.

And three days later he did indeed pass out from the life which he had loved so well, and had laid down so lovingly.

The Water-carrier claims his reward

The King who kept his Word

There is one story told of Humayun, the Moon-Lady's son, which is worth remembering.

Sher Khan, the Afghan, turned traitor, and the King was compelled to fly for his life. But there was no escape except across a river in flood; and his horse sank exhausted in mid-stream. Then the King would have died; but a water-carrier on the opposite bank saw the King's trouble, and brought him his own skin-bags, on which Humayun floated safely to land.

"I have nothing to give thee now," said the King; "but come to me in Agra, and if I live thou shalt sit on my throne for a whole day." The King did live, and got back his kingdom; and the water-carrier came to claim his reward.

Humayun kept his word, like the King that he was.

For one whole day the water-carrier sat on the throne; and the skin that had saved the King's life was cut into little pieces and stamped into money by the Royal Mint.

Naila

Ghyas-ud-din Tughlak, the Moghul, had heard of the beauty of the daughters of Rana-Mal-Bhatti, the Rajput: and he wished a Rajput princess for the wife of his brother Rajab.

But when he sent to ask this, Rana Mal made a haughty answer—"No daughter of the Moon could wed with a slayer of cows."

Then Tughlak demanded at once, and in cash, a whole year's tribute to be paid to Delhi. And Rana Mal was sad, for though the people stripped themselves bare, it would not be easy.

And the sound of the people's crying reached the ears of Rana Mal's old mother, who came to her son's house weeping, with unbound hair, to plead for the people. And as she came Naila, the most beautiful of Rana

Mal's daughters, saw her and ran to open the door to her.

"Why weeps my grandmother?" asked Naila.

"Because of you," said the old woman. "The Turk is taxing our people, because your father will not give you in marriage to the Turk as he desires."

"If to give me to the Turk will save our people," said Naila, "send me at once, grandmother. Think only that the robber Turks have carried off one of your jewels." So did Naila give herself for her country.

And afterwards her only son Firoz Shah served his people in the same spirit. He was loved by them all. Cruelty gave place to kindness, taking to giving, hating to loving—and for thirty-seven years there was peace and prosperity and goodwill in Delhi.

The Lotus-Lady

In the days when Ala-ud-din, the Moslem, ruled at Delhi, the beautiful rock-fortress Chittore was the capital of Rajputana, and brave Prince Bhimsi was regent for his nephew the Baby-King.

Now Bhimsi had a most beautiful wife, the Lotus-Lady, the fame of whose beauty had gone forth all over India. And in the old days men thought it not wrong to try and snatch away from others anything which they wished to possess—be this thing what it might, rich city or lovely lady or priceless jewel.

So Ala-ud-din waged war on Chittore in order to capture the lovely Lotus-Lady. But the Rajput warriors laughed him to scorn, and defeated him, and kept safe their beauteous Lady of the Lotus.

Then Ala-ud-din pretended to be very much ashamed that he had ever even imagined that Prince Bhimsi would let the Princess be taken captive by an enemy.

"But," he added, "I have come a long way and have fought hard, and you have conquered. Therefore before I go, let me look, I pray, but for one minute on the beauty of which I have heard so much.

"Let me see the face of the Princess Lady, just for a breathing-space, not openly, but in a mirror—so that I may have in my soul a vision of the Perfectly Beautiful, to help me in the days that remain."

And Bhimsi was so noble a knight that he was moved by these words to grant his enemy his desire.

Ala-ud-din pretended to be very grateful, and the courteous knight Bhimsi was sorry for the enemy whom he had defeated. Thinking him to be also a knight and bound by knightly courtesies and honour, he accompanied him alone outside the gates of the city, to set him on his way.

But when Ala-ud-din got Bhimsi alone and at his mercy, he carried him captive to his own camp. Only in exchange for the Lotus-Lady herself, he declared, would he release the Rajput Prince-Regent.

Then all the knights and warriors of Chittore took counsel with the Princess as to what should be done. And the Lotus-Lady was brave: for she loved her lord very dearly.

So in concert with her nobles, she arranged that word should be sent to Ala-ud-din that she was coming, as he

The Lotus-Lady at the prisoner's tent

commanded, to release her lord: but that she craved a few minutes' speech of her lord, before parting with him for ever. And Ala-ud-din granted her request.

So, for the camp of the enemy set forth a great procession of palanquins and mace-bearers; and Ala-ud-din was not afraid, for he knew that so great a lady might not be abroad without her waiting-women and her mistresses of the robes, and her mace-bearers and the slaves who did her bidding—one slave for each separate little duty of the care of her lovely person.

And now the Lotus-Lady was at the prisoner's tent of her lord; and now she had bid him farewell, and the long line of palanquins had turned once more towards Chittore.

And Ala-ud-din said: "Ha! now will I have both the Prince and his bride!"

and he ordered the palanquins to stop, thinking to make an easy capture of the prisoner whom he had just exchanged, among the palanquins of the women-folk.

But the warriors of Chittore had prepared a surprise for Ala-ud-din, the traitor. Forth from every palanquin streamed the bravest of Chittore's Rajput knights—the very palanquin-bearers were warriors: and they fought and routed Ala-ud-din and his hosts, and carried their Prince and his lady safely to the palace of their fortress home.

And Ala-ud-din fled in haste to Delhi.

But Ala-ud-din never forgot this second disgrace. Nor, it is said, could he forget the face of the Lotus-Lady.

He must have been a bad man indeed, and no knight at all, in that even the vision of Perfect Beauty had not the power to kill in him that which was base and self-seeking. So yet once more, he sallied forth against Chittore long years afterwards, when the Baby-King was full grown, and with his twelve brave sons, and Bhimsi, and the other brave Rajput princes, kept faithful guard over the honour of knighthood in Rajputana.

And Ala-ud-din took with him mighty armies and great engines of war, and by sheer force of numbers and deadly weapons he bore down the brave little body of knights fighting on the walls of their beloved city.

Then again the knights sat in council. "Our weak and defenceless ones shall not," they said, "fall into the hands of a coward enemy."

And they took their women down into the vaults beneath the city, where the Rajput woman was wont to go through fire to meet her lord who had died in battle. And they left them enough wood and fire for the sacrifice.

And the women wore their most beautiful garments, to walk down to the vaults, a long line of beauty and courage led by the queen of beauty, the Lotus-Lady herself.

And now it was the turn of the men. And the King and his sons and his brave knights all strove as to who should be first to meet single-handed the enemy at the gates. And they cast lots: and went one by one clad in the Rajput saffron robe of conquest: and single-handed each hewed his way through the gates, strewing the moat and outworks with the bodies of the slain.

But Ayeshi, his beloved son, had the King sent secretly beforehand to a place of safety, that the race of warriors might still continue. And when night fell, the last of the Rajputs had left the city, having laid, each man, at the feet of the true knight and champion of the defenceless, a full sheaf of the unknightly ones.

And Ala-ud-din came walking carefully across this carpet of the dead, into a fortress of which the gates were wide. But no man nor woman nor child found he anywhere in Chittore. All was emptiness—palace and hut, and bathing-ghat, and council chamber, and garden and marble-latticed roof—empty, all empty.

Then at last did he realize that what was in his hands was not victory but defeat; and that the beauty and goodness of which we are not worthy, may not, in this life or the next, be taken by violence.

The Perfect Host

Rasmal Rana of Marwar had three sons—Sanga, Prithi Raj, and Jismal. And Prithi Raj was ambitious, and would boast that Fate meant him to lead the sons of Marwar.

One day when he was boasting on this wise his eldest brother Sanga said:

"Let the gods decide between us, brother. Although I am the eldest, you are welcome to my birthright, if so it is written. At the Tiger's Mount lives the priestess who sees the future. Let us ask her who is to lead the ten thousand towns of Marwar when our father is dead."

So they rode on together to the Tiger's Mount. The cave was empty, and they sat down to await the priestess.

The cave was simply furnished—a bed, a panther's skin, a beggar's bowl of water. Prithi Raj made for the bed, but Sanga sought the hearth-rug.

And the priestess entered and looked at Sanga.

"In olden times," she said, "the panther's skin was the seat of princes. As now you sit on this skin, so one day shall you sit on the throne of Marwar."

At this Prithi Raj drew his sword and would have slain his brother, but their uncle stepped between, and Sanga escaped.

He rode hard, his horse bleeding from sword-thrusts, for Jismal, his younger brother, was after him, while the uncle engaged Prithi Raj.

A long way from the mount he came upon a very holy sanctuary. At its gates stood Rahtore Beeda, the perfect host: his horse stood beside him ready for a journey.

"Nay—not while he is my guest"

"I am Sanga, son of Rasmal Rana: my brothers seek to kill me," said Sanga.

"Have no fear," said Rahtore Beeda. "I will defend the sanctuary while you get away. See, there is my horse."

And even as he spoke his eyes travelled to the speck of dust on the horizon.

And now Jismal and his men had come up. But Rahtore Beeda stood alone at the door of the sanctuary.

"We want Sanga."

"He is my guest."

"Then let us seek for him."

"Nay—not while he is my guest," said Rahtore Beeda, the perfect host, drawing his sword.

Alone he stood against them. And when at last they forced their way into the sanctuary over his dead body, Sanga was far away in safety.

And the perfect host had kept his tradition of hospitality.

The Dove-Girl and the Prince

There was once a Persian Prince of noble birth who lost all his money: so he left his country and came to India, bringing with him his wife and three children.

"It will not", he said, "be so hard to be poor in a strange country."

He travelled with a great many other people, all coming through the snow mountains and passes, and wild bleak places of Afghanistan. The women rode on camels, slung in cages on either side of the driver; and most of their luggage also was carried in this way. The men walked, and the journey took a weary long time for man and beast. The travellers halted to cook their food, and they halted again to sleep by great watch-fires, till the dawn-star told them that it was time to go on once more.

One day a baby was born to the wife of the Persian, and he was very cross. "It is only a girl," he said, "and no use at all." So when no one was looking he laid it on the grass by the roadside, and meant to go away and leave it there to die.

Now it happened that a great man known at the Court of the Emperor Akbar, was also travelling with the pilgrims for safety; for there were many robbers in those days, and only if a man travelled with a crowd of people in what was called a Caravan, could he be safe.

And the great man saw the poor little baby lying alone on the grass, and, as it seemed to belong to no one, he said he would take it for his own. And he looked about among the

The second dove also flew happily away

women in the Caravan for a nurse.

And the baby's mother came forward and said: "Please let me be nurse." So the baby had its own mother after all to care for it.

Now the great man from Akbar's Court was so kind that the woman told him all her story, and he asked to see her husband and her sons, and sent them all to the Emperor himself for protection. So it came to pass that the man from Persia got work and honour at the Emperor's Court.

And the baby born by the roadside grew very beautiful, and was called *Mihr-un-Nisa*, which means "the Sun of Womankind". She lived near the Palace, and would go with the women into the Palace gardens, whenever the great Fairs took place, where the zenana women sold their lovely work and embroideries.

And at one of these Fairs, Prince Salim, the Emperor's son, lost his way in an empty part of the garden, where he could see no one but a small girl at play. He had in his hands his two favourite doves, and, wanting to fly kites with the boys at the fair, he told the little girl, who was our "Sun of Womankind", to hold the doves till he should return. "Take care," he said; "don't let them fly."

When he came back *Mihr-un-Nisa* had only one dove in her hands.

"Where is the other?" said Prince Salim.

"I let it fly," said *Mihr-un-Nisa.*

And, "How did you do that, stupid-one?" said the Prince angrily.

"Just so, my Prince," said *Mihr-un-Nisa*, opening her other hand, from which the second dove also flew happily away.

She looked so beautiful in her naughtiness that the Prince fell in love with her that minute. And many years afterwards, when he became Emperor, he married her, and changed her name to *Nŭr Mahal*, "the Light of the Palace". And again, for she seemed more beautiful still to him every day, he changed it to *Nŭr Jehan*, "the Light of the World".

And her lovely face is still to be seen painted on ivory and vellum among the treasures of the ancient city of Delhi.

The Boy who was Always Thirteen

There were once a man and woman so truly good that the great god said he would reward them with whatever they wished to ask. "We want a son," said the man and his wife.

"You shall have a son," said Shiva, the great god. "But you must now choose the kind of son you want. Will you have him perfect in every way, beautiful and good and clever, and loved by all the world, but doomed to be no older than his thirteenth year? Or will you have him just an ordinary boy, but living as long as the ordinary man, so that you may even see his children's children? Choose: that which you wish shall be given."

And the man and his wife were sorrowful; for to choose was not easy.

How could they bear their son to die when he was thirteen. Yet how could they bear to have him just an ordinary boy, like any other that came into the world, and had trouble, and made mistakes, and died at last, leaving no name behind him? And the puzzle was too hard for the man.

"I cannot choose," he said to his wife. "You must decide. It is your business."

And the woman said: "We will have the perfect son that Shiva has offered us. And the rest we will leave to the gods."

So Kamil, the perfect one, was born, and grew from happy baby to happy boy. And he was beautiful to look upon; and clever was he, and strong, and gentle, and kind. Everyone loved him, and to all gave he love also, making happiness wherever he went.

And his father and mother, and all the people of his village, alike forgot that there could be any end to this happiness. But the King of Death did not forget. "No older than his thirteenth year," had said Shiva, the great god. And Kamil, the perfect boy, was in his thirteenth year.

So, on his birthday, the King of Death sent his messengers, to bring Kamil away to the Kingdom of Death. "It is only another kind of life," said the messengers; "do not be afraid, come with us. The King himself is waiting to receive you."

But the boy said: "Why should I come? I want no other kind of life. This life I love. Why should I come? I will not come with you."

"No one has ever disobeyed the King of Death," said the messengers. "Come, you must."

"I will not come," said the boy. "Go back to the King of Death and say: 'The boy who loves the life he knows, says that he cannot come to the new life which he does not know.'"

And the messengers went trembling back to the King with this message.

Now the King of Death is very old, and very kind and gentle, and he has the wisdom of Peace and of Forgetfulness. And the journey back to the life which the boy loved was for him a very long journey. "But I must see," he said, "the one person who has disobeyed me." So he sent for his black buffalo, and he rode the long and painful journey back to Life and Youth in the world of the-things-that-pass.

And it was spring-time, and the leaves of the pipal tree were shining after a shower of rain, which had made

"I am Death, who sent to fetch you"

all the world smell sweet with the good earth-smell. And the birds were singing. And under the pipal tree stood the perfect boy beside the shrine of Shiva, the great god, playing a little tune of the gladness of the-things-that-pass.

He played on a slender reed of bamboo, blowing with his mouth; and he called the cattle to come home to rest, for it was the cow-dust hour, and the sun was setting.

When the King of Death was close by the perfect boy stopped playing, and looked at him riding on the long, long back of his slow-moving grey-black buffalo.

"What an old, old man you are!" said the perfect boy; "never have I seen you before. Who are you?"

"You have seen my messengers," said the King. "I am Death, who sent to fetch you to my kingdom. Why did you not come?"

"I told your messengers," said the boy. "It was quite true. It is very kind of you to want to take me to your kingdom; but I do not wish any other life. I love this life very much, and I am so happy. I love my father and my mother, and all the men-and-women people, and the children-people, and the beast-people, and bird-people in this good life that I know. You stay with us too. See, I will ask my mother to make room for you in our own little hut." But the King of Death shook his head.

"I have a kingdom, and I come to take you to it. Come, make no trouble. Get up behind me on the buffalo; we must be back before to-morrow's day."

"And I say again, I will not come,"

said the boy, standing firm. "See, I appeal to Shiva to protect me;" and he put out his hand to the large pebble of black stone, Shiva's symbol, which had been brought to the shrine from the great sacred river of the West Country.

Then the King of Death was angry, and he laid hands on the boy to take him by force; and he dragged him away, so that the symbol of Shiva fell to the ground.

And now Shiva himself, the great god, was angered, and his voice thundered forth, ordering the King of Death back to the Kingdom of Death. "And you shall not return to the world of the-things-that-pass, till I bid you," said Shiva.

So back went the old king on his slow-moving, grey-black buffalo. And the boy was happy, and life was again full of love and goodness as before, in his world of the-things-that-pass.

But the King of Death could no more send his messengers to the Earth; so everything lived forever—the men and women and beasts and birds and flower-people all lived; and yet new men and women and beasts and birds and flower-people were always coming to the Earth, as before. So that the Earth was fuller than it could hold.

And the men and women and beasts and birds and flower-people went to the great god and said: "We are weary, and there is no room for us on the Earth; we are the things that must pass. Send the King of Death to take us to the Kingdom of Peace and Forgetfulness and Quiet Sleep."

And the great god said: "I will not; I have spoken."

Then the tired Earth-people went to

Parvati, the wife of Shiva, and, "Please help us," they said. "See how full the Earth is. There is no room for us all, and some of us are weary and would sleep."

So Parvati went to the great god. "The Earth is very full," she said. "Will you not let the King of Death send his slow-moving grey-black buffalo for the tired Earth-people?"

"No," said Shiva; "he insulted my symbol: he may not return to the Earth. I have spoken."

"But you know you did say that the perfect boy was to be no older than his thirteenth year," said Parvati. "That was why the King of Death came to fetch him."

And Shiva was silent, not knowing what to answer.

"But when you said that, you only meant that he should never look older than his thirteenth year, though he might live and live as long as he liked," said clever goddess Parvati.

And Shiva waited, for surely here was a way out of a difficulty.

"And poor old King Death was not clever enough to understand this, and thought that you meant him to take the boy away. It was only stupidity. Forgive him."

And Shiva said: "It shall be as you ask."

"Then give the message," said Goddess Parvati.

And, "Let the old tired leaves fall from the trees," said Shiva the god, and turned to other business.

But his messengers were so full of gladness that good King Death might return to the Earth once more, riding on his grey-black buffalo—for that was the meaning of Shiva's message—that they were drunk with joy, and said the words wrongly.

"Let the old leaves, and the middle-aged leaves, and the little baby leaves fall from the trees," was what they said, when they flew back to the Earth on the wings of the morning.

And that is why to this day, old and young, boys and babies, all alike, ride, when the great god wills, upon the grey-black buffalo, as it makes its slow-moving way to the quiet Kingdom of Death.

But Kamil, the perfect boy, lived in the world that he loved, and was always and always just thirteen years old, and no more.

And, "It was well," said the man, his father, "that I left the Son-puzzle to you, O Mother of Kamil."